MW01061985

COME FOR CHOLENT

Cast bronze *cholent* pot, Frankfort, 1582. The inscription shows that it belonged to Hirtz Popper's wife, daugher of Moses Zur Leiter. Jewish Museum / Art Resource, N.Y.

COME FOR CHOLENT

•The Jewish Stew Cookbook•

Kay Kantor Pomerantz

Bloch Publishing Company
New York

Manufactured in the United States of America

Third Printing

Library of Congress Cataloging-in-Publication Data

Pomerantz, Kay Kantor.
    Come for *cholent*: the Jewish stew cookbook /by
Kay Kantor Pomerantz.
        p. cm.
        ISBN: 0-8197-0598-5 : $8.95
        1. Stews.   2. Cookery, Jewish.   I. Title.
        TX693.P66   1991   91-35294
        641.8'23--dc20   CIP

A clan and a family resemble a heap of stones: one stone taken out of it and the whole totters.

Genesis Rabbah

חֲבוּרָה וּמִשְׁפָּחָה דוֹמִין לְכִפַּת אֲבָנִים: אַתָּה נוֹטֵל מִמֶּנָּה אֶבֶן אַחַת וְכֻלָּה מִתְרוֹעַעַת

בראשית רבה ק

In memory of my beloved parents, Jake and Goldie Kantor, my brother, Bernard Kantor, and niece, Kathie Kantor Young.

With special thanks to my loving family -- my husband Moshe, Raquel and Bill, Benjamin Jacob and Eliana Zehava, Alisa and Stephen, Ari and Joey. May good health and length of days, happiness and laughter, and the time to enjoy them, be theirs in abundance.

Remember: A family that cholents together, sticks together!

Special thanks to Tom Funk, staff artist of the *Dramatists Guild Quarterly*, whose work appears in *The New Yorker*, children's books and greeting cards, for his many drawings throughout this book.

i

About the Title

COME FOR *CHOLENT*!

Come For *Cholent* -- Those three little words represent the most concise invitation ever extended. They even describe what's on the menu.

Although Jewish law prohibits kindling a fire on *Shabbat* (the Jewish Sabbath, from sundown Friday to sundown Saturday) it is nevertheless considered a *mitzvah* (a good deed) to eat a hot meal at midday on Saturday. In fact, over the centuries, Jews throughout the world have worked out a number of ingenious solutions for this dilemma. All involve food cooking overnight at a very low heat. In the past, a hot fire was started in the baker's oven (or home oven) before *Shabbat* and then left to slowly cook itself out over a long period of time. In order to keep the *Cholent* warm, it is partially cooked in a heavy pot on Friday -- half or at least one-third cooked -- and then a short while before *Shabbat* placed in a low oven, on a *blech* (a metal sheet placed over a low fire) on top of the stove, or more recently acceptable, in a crock pot, until it is ready to be used. *Cholent* was and is a favorite *Shabbat* dish because its flavor is improved by long, slow cooking. It may be served as a main course or as a side dish. Its consistency when done is thick, without liquid, but not quite dry.

So, an invitation to come over for *cholent* clearly designates Saturday lunch.

There's no way of predicting in advance (unless you're the cook) what type of *Cholent* will be served. Traditional *cholent* is a tasty dish that includes meat and meat bones, potatoes, barley and often several types of beans in a variety of combinations. It may also be prepared vegetarian style without meat of any kind. Interestingly, *Cholent* is eaten by Jews everywhere in the world. It is rich in flavor, full of nutrition and exquisite in its simplicity of preparation. With a bit of *mazel* -- good luck -- perhaps your invitation will be for one of the tasty *Cholent*s included in this book. There is nothing comparable to entering one's home (or that of family or friends) where the wonderful aroma of *Cholent* simmering in the oven greets you.

This book is intended to help you extend the invitation to "Come For *Cholent*" often. May you also have the good fortune of being invited to

Come For *Cholent!*

TABLE OF CONTENTS

About the Title   ii

   Dear Reader   1

   Important Information For All   3
   Cholent Recipes

   Very Basic Scrumptious *Cholent*   5

I   *Cholent* With Accompaniments   7

II   Vegetarian *Cholent*   13
     FYI -- Or a Little Knowledge....   14

III *Cholent* By Color   19
     Cholent "Talk"   20

IV   Meat Specialties   23
     That Special Spice   24

V   International *Cholent*   37
     Cholent Notes   38

VI   Very Special *Cholent*   55
     Regional Cooking in America   56

VII Exotic *Cholent*   63
     The *Cholent* Challenge   64
     Cholent Previews   65

VIII Miscellaneous *Cholent*   73
     P.S.   74

Dear Reader:

I dedicate this volume to all those who love to eat and prefer to cook "easy to prepare" meals. *Cholent* is a complete meal in a pot. I used to think *cholent* was *cholent* and there was only one way to make it. I've since learned there are as many versions of *cholent* as there are cooks. Basically *cholent* is any combination of food that has the stamina to withstand 24 hours of cooking! As a true chocolate lover as well as a *cholent* afficionado, my only frustration is in having only one recipe that includes chocolate. Otherwise I could have called this book Chocolate *cholent* -- what a great title!

The proverbial expression "what you put in, you get out" applies very much to *cholent*. *Cholent* planning comes AFTER the choice of ingredients, not before it. That is, create your *cholent* based on what is fresh and available.

This cookbook is also for all those who are able to face traditional Jewish cooking with a sense of humor. Reading these pages may not provide a thorough historical overview but it should provide endless hours of *Shabbat* sustenance and conversation. Besides, sharing and comparing *cholent* recipes is always good grist for a hearty laugh!

While gathering these recipes and preparing these pages I had many dreams. Some of them were sincere -- such as engendering a love of *cholent* in all people and therefore a return to, and embracing of, the celebration of *Shabbat*. Some were ludicrous -- such as walking along and stepping down into a quicksand-like beach of *cholent*.

At one point I began to obsess over *cholent*. I imagined that my sons were in the kitchen molding it into softballs for a game of *cholent*ball. My husband delivered his greatest sermon ever, The Joys of Judaism -- Children and *Cholent*. Barbra Streisand sang, "I'm In a *Cholent* Frame of Mind."

When asked by my "nearest and dearest" why I was writing this book, I gave many responses. Basically, I felt it had to be done -- and no one else I knew would do it. I also wanted to connect with *Cholent* afficionados throughout our history. And, last, but most important, the educator in me sensed a golden opportunity to reach people.

Many have suggested a *Come For Cholent* sequel -- sharing *cholent* stories and anecdotes. If you are interested, please write to me care of the publisher and include your best stories.

Very special thanks to all who survived the challenge of my *cholent* chatter! To Dorothy Nathan, brilliant computer whiz, and to readers Ruth Bovanick, Rabbi Shelley Melzer and Dorothy Sachs. Thanks also to all who shared their recipes and memories and to all those who were willing tasters!

IMPORTANT INFORMATION FOR ALL
CHOLENT RECIPES

• All *cholent* recipes will feed a minimum of 4 to 6 hungry eaters as a main course, but can be stretched to feed many more as a side dish.

• *Cholent* may be made in a crock pot, a heavy pot set on stove top *blech* (a sheet of metal placed over a low fire) or in the oven. Prior to *Shabbat*, oven temperature should be reduced to $200\text{-}250^0$.

• As *cholent* is served traditionally for Saturday lunch, please note: Winter *cholent* cooks longer than summer *cholent*, therefore you must adjust the water level accordingly (more water is needed in winter where *Shabbat* begins as early as 4 in the afternoon). In fact, most favor *cholent* in the winter as it is a hot and filling dish!

• Hints to soften beans for easy digetion: Beans should be picked over and rinsed with cold water. They may be prepared for cooking by either soaking for 4 hours; soaking overnight, or pre-boiled for 5 minutes and then allowed to stand covered for one hour. Follow preparation by rinsing beans with cold water. Optional: A small slice of seaweed may be added as a natural tenderizer.

• Water or liquid level should be high enough to cover all ingredients and no higher than within an inch of the top of the pot. All recipes list "water" but do not specify exact amounts.

• After the water begins to boil, skim off froth as it rises to the surface.

• A few hours before lunch, check the *cholent*: If it is too moist, uncover it and leave it in the oven to dry. Correct the seasoning as desired.

• The amount of salt and pepper to use is delineated in the Very Basic Scrumptious *Cholent*, but is really intended as a taste tester's guide. Thereafter, all recipes have "salt and pepper" only, with no amount specified. Please season according to taste. Do not oversalt. Additional salt may be added when served.

• *Cholent* brings out creativity and originality in most cooks. Experiment, improvise and enjoy!

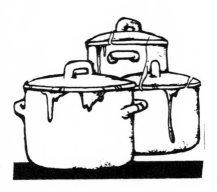

VERY BASIC SCRUMPTIOUS *CHOLENT*

1/2 cup medium
  barley
1/2 cup small white,
  baby lima beans
1/2 cup red kidney
  beans
6 small red potatoes
1 1/2 lbs. flanken, cut
  into large chunks
5 or 6 beef marrow or
  neck bones

1 onion, chopped fine
2 cloves garlic, chopped
  fine or put through a
  press
2 T. oil
cold water
approx. 2 t. salt
1 t. black pepper,
  freshly ground

Brown meat and onions in oil in saucepan (or place meat and onions beneath oven broiler for a few minutes). Rinse barley in a sieve under cold running water, until water runs clear. Pick over beans and rinse thoroughly. Peel potatoes and cut into rounds. Add barley, beans, potatoes, bones, and garlic to meat and onions in the saucepan. Add 6-7 cups cold water, or enough to cover, and bring to a boil over high heat. Season with salt and pepper and simmer for one hour. Skim froth as it rises to the surface. Place in oven as indicated in preface.

•Cholent, *pronounced "tsoh-lent"* •
The origin of the word cholent *may have come from the old French word* chald, *which meant warm. The Hebrew name for* cholent *is* hamim *which means "hot."*

CHAPTER I

CHOLENT WITH ACCOMPANIMENTS

Cholent with *Kishke*
Kishke Variations for *Cholent*
Cholent with *Knaidle*
The *Ganef Knaidle*
Cholent with *Kugel*
Cholent with *Hallah Kugel*

• A Jewish philosophical aside goes: "If you cannot afford chicken, herring will do." Please don't follow this precept for making *cholent*!

CHOLENT WITH KISHKE

This recipe works well on its own but is particularly delicious with any of your favorite accompaniments such as kishke, knaidlach, *or* kugel.

6 small potatoes	1/2 cup navy beans
1 lb. meat, cubed	salt & pepper (to taste)
1 onion, sliced	garlic (fresh or pow-
1/2 cup kidney beans	der)
1/2 cup small lima	1 cup minced carrots
beans	and celery

Peel potatoes and cut in halves. Rinse meat and beans and place with onion in a large pot. Add water and seasonings.

Bring to a boil and then reduce heat and simmer. To start, keep pot uncovered and keep adding water as necessary. Once the beans have expanded they won't absorb the water as rapidly. Prior to *Shabbat* be sure there is water at least 1" above ingredients.

Add *kishke* (several recipes follow on the next page). Cover the pot tightly and cook in desired manner.

KISHKE VARIATIONS FOR CHOLENT

Originally, kishke *was made from a length of cow intestine that had been cleaned, salted, then stuffed with a variant of the* kishke *mix below. The open end of the* kishke *was sewn with thread and baked. In today's world of synthetic products, most commecially sold* kishke *uses a thin plastic casing instead of intestine. Here's a recipe for making your own.*

BASIC:
1/2 cup oil   1 1/2 cup flour*
2 stalks celery   1 t. paprika
2 carrots   salt & pepper to taste
1 onion

Blend 1/2 cup oil and cut-up vegetables in blender or food processor until it becomes a thick paste. Empty into bowl and add seasonings. Mix well. Form into a roll and place on a large piece of greased aluminum foil and seal tightly. If desired you may place on top of the food in the *cholent* to cook with it or bake separately on a cookie sheet for 1-1 1/2 hours at 360⁰ then save, slice and serve with *cholent*. (It may be left in cholent until served.)

*CRACKER *KISHKE*: Substitute 1 box (8 oz.) of crackers for flour.

CHOLENT WITH KNAIDLE

1 cup *matzah* meal   2 T. cold water
1 T. oil   2 eggs, beaten
                         salt

Beat eggs slightly with fork. Add other ingredients, except *matzah* meal, and mix. Add *matzah* meal gradually until thick. Stir well. Refrigerate in covered bowl for 15-20 minutes. Form into large ball and add to *cholent* after it has come to a full boil so that *knaidle* won't sink to bottom. Leave in pot until *cholent* is served.

THE *GANEF KNAIDLE*

One hundred years ago, the huge dumpling, known today as the knaidle, *was called a* ganef -- a thief -- *when it was cooked in the* Shabbat cholent. *It received this title because the coarse lump of dough stole succulent flavors from the fat, the meat and the vegetables in the pot, to emerge enriched, puffed, and delightful upon the festive table.*

3/4 cup self-rising flour   1 egg, beaten
1/4 cup semolina   3 T. water
salt & pepper (to taste)   1/2 cup fat or oil
                            dash of ginger

Mix all the ingredients together and put the resulting lump of dough into the *cholent* after the other ingredients have come to a boil. Let the *ganef* stew in the juice of its "neighbor" as long as it cooks!

CHOLENT WITH *KUGEL*

1 medium diced onion
1 cup oil
1 egg

salt & pepper (to taste)
paprika
enough flour to form a
dough

Mix all ingredients just until blended. Refrigerate for a few hours. Shape into a loaf and place in *cholent* that is already boiling.

CHOLENT WITH *ḤALLAH KUGEL*

1 medium-size *hallah*
(1 lb.)
2-3 eggs

1 onion, chopped
finely
salt & pepper (to taste)

Soak and drain the *hallah*. Mix in other ingredients. Roll up in aluminum foil and place on top of *cholent*.

CHAPTER II

VEGETARIAN CHOLENT

4 Variations

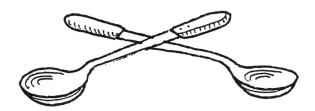

"Life is a lot like a *cholent*. You mix in a lot of things and never quite know the outcome."

FYI -- OR, A LITTLE KNOWLEDGE IS A GOOD THING!

Kasha -- Roasted buckwheat groats. Most people are surprised to learn that groats are not a grain but fruit related botanically to rhubarb. It is a plant that prospers in climates and areas where growing wheat is not possible. It is high in protein, B vitamins, iron and calcium and highly nutritious.

Lima Beans -- Limas come from Peru (Lima is the capital) and date back some 7500 years. How they left the Americas and showed up in Eastern European shtetls is still a puzzle to me. The small size cook more rapidly than the larger size beans but taste exactly the same. After soaking the beans, I prefer rubbing them between my fingers to remove the skins. This is certainly not required but produces a smoother texture. (It could be likened to the preference for creamy peanut butter versus the chunky style.)

Chick Peas -- Chick peas are high in protein, calcium, iron and B vitamins and are very healthful. Called garbanzo beans in Spanish and ceci in Italian, they've been around a very long time.

Lentils -- Lentils may be the oldest cultivated legume. Ever since Esau sold his birthright for a dish of stewed lentils, they have been feeding the hungry of this world. They are totally lacking in fat and have lots of minerals and vitamins. All lentils should be picked over to remove small stones and grit and washed through a colander several times.

They don't need to be soaked. They are always filling and highly nutritious.

Barley -- It may be helpful to know that barley expands when cooked and even expands after it's cooked! Always use a light touch when adding barley to *cholent* recipes and watch it grow. In some countries, I'm told, it's thrown at the bride and groom, in place of rice, to encourage fertility.

Garlic -- Some feel garlic is a potent aphrodisiac and also wards off sickness when hung around the neck. There's more about garlic in the section on regional *cholents*. Frankly, I enjoyed it before I realized how good it is for you!

I. VEGETARIAN *CHOLENT*

6 potatoes
1 onion, cut in rings
2-3 stalks of celery
4-5 carrots

8 oz. tomato sauce
salt & pepper (to taste)
water

Layer bottom of pot with onion rings. Then add celery, carrot and potatoes. Add seasonings, tomato sauce and enough water to cover. Cook for approximately one hour before *Shabbat* and place in oven, on the *blech* or in the crock pot.

II. VEGETARIAN *CHOLENT* WITH TOFU

Add one package smooth tofu cut in 1 1/2 inch chunks, to vegetarian *cholent*. Bring water level to within one inch of top of pot.

I tried this recipe adding one small peeled eggplant (cubed, salted and drained for 30 minutes). It rated high marks even from my ravenous teenage sons!

III. CURRIED *CHOLENT* .

A favorite of the incredible Kellner clan of Westchester.

4 cubed potatoes
2 cubed sweet potatoes
2 zucchini (cut in rounds)
1 onion, diced
2 T. oil

1 cup mixed beans
1 cup large lima beans
2 t. curry powder
salt & pepper (to taste)
water

Add all ingredients saving sufficient zucchini rounds to form a circle around *cholent*. Cover tightly.

IV. VEGETARIAN *CHOLENT* (SWEET)

This recipe is dedicated to The Schillers of Mercer Island.

2-3 sweet potatoes*
1 large onion
1 turnip (optional)
2 stalks celery
2 carrots
1 potato
1 1/2 cups mixed
    beans

1/2 cup brown rice
4-5 dates (chopped)
1 T. oil
water
Season with garlic,
    cinnamon, honey,
    soy sauce, salt and
    pepper

Cut vegetables into large chunks and saute in oil. Add rice, beans and water to cover. When beans are soft add dates and season "to taste."

*Summer or winter squash makes a tasty addition. You may substitute it or use in combination with sweet potatoes.

CHAPTER III

CHOLENT BY COLOR

Red *Cholent*
White *Cholent*
Green *Cholent*

• Heinrich Heine wrote of the *cholent* eaten at a friend's home in Frankfurt: "True to Jewish custom, he placed a dish of the traditional *cholent* before me at the Sabbath noon. I liked the ancient dish enormously: it perhaps dates back to the Jewish sojourn in Egypt and is as old as the Pyramids... With what savour, with what delight and eagerness, with what appetite, I polished off this age-old Jewish dish of *cholent*!?"

CHOLENT "TALK"

CHOLENT makes a strong statement and is the opposite of non-chalant!

CHOLENT comes from two words -- chow (to eat a lot) and lent (from whatever ingredients my neighbor lent me!)

Chawlint -- Litvak pronunciation
Chilent -- Galitzianer pronunciation
Shulent -- Yekeh pronunciation
Chewnt --Missouri pronunciation
Cholentr -- Bostonian pronunciation

CHOLENT sticks to your ribs, right between your cholenders!

CHOLENT is to a flu what chicken soup is to a cold!

C-is for Cholent, of course!
H-eaten on the Holy Sabbath
O-One serving will suffice
L-Later you'll remember you've eaten beans!
E-Energized you'll feel
N-Never more than once a week
T-the Tastiest dish, having passed the Test of Time!

CHOLENT has seven letters ending on the 7th and therefore eaten on the seventh day, Shabbat. CHOLENT -- has HOLE in the middle, for the *knaidle*! And is therefore somehow related to the bagel!

RED *CHOLENT*

My teenage sons, Ari and Joey, agree that this is their favorite cholent! *What do they know, they could dine on pizza nightly! It's probably the ketchup in this recipe that turns them on!*

1 large onion
5-6 potatoes
1/2 cup barley
1 1/2 cup navy beans
  (or baked beans in
  tomato sauce)

2 oz. ketchup
1 lb. chuck roast (cut
  up)
meat bones (optional)
water
salt & pepper (to
  taste)

Slice onion thinly and place on bottom of a 3-quart pot. Add potatoes cut in halves or quarters. Add barley, beans, meat and bones. It is not necessary to stir. Add enough water to cover all ingredients. Add seasonings. Cook for one hour prior to *Shabbat*.

WHITE *CHOLENT*

Same as red except replace ketchup with one can condensed mushroom soup -- delicious!

GREEN *CHOLENT*

4 lbs. pot roast
1 can tomato slices
1 large white onion,
  sliced
6 small red potatoes,
  peeled

4 T. dried or fresh
  parsley
1 T. cilantro (coriander)
1/2 cup green peppers
1/2 cup green zucchini
salt & pepper (to taste)
water to cover

Place meat, vegetables and potatoes in large pot. Add seasonings, parsley, cilantro and water. Cover and place in oven. Additional fresh parsley may be added when serving.

CHAPTER IV

MEAT SPECIALTIES

Sweet and Sour Meatball *Cholent*
Boiled Beef *Cholent*
Lamb *Cholent*
Raquel's *Cholent* with Brisket
Sweet and Sour Tongue *Cholent*
Sausage *Cholent*
Shoulder of Lamb *Cholent*
Hamburger *Cholent*
Pine Nut *Cholent*
Chicken and *Kasha Cholent*
Veal *Cholent*
Pupik *Cholent*
"Spare Parts" *Cholent*
Turkey *Cholent*
Duck *Cholent*

"If you eat *cholent* for 90 years you'll live a long time."

That Special Spice!

An interesting story is related in the Talmud (*Shabbat* 113a) about the special fragrance, taste and flavor of *cholent*. It seems a certain Roman Emperor used to visit quite frequently with Rabbi Yehoshua ben Hananiah. The Rabbi and Emperor would converse for long hours on important matters. Occasionally, the Emperor would visit on *Shabbat* (the Sabbath) and would be particularly delighted when served up a steaming hot bowl of delicious *cholent*. He pleaded with the Rabbi for the recipe time and time again. But when the Rabbi finally gave it to him, he told him that it wouldn't taste the same since its preparation involved the use of a certain spice that wasn't available to anyone else. The emperor returned to his palace to give the recipe to his great chefs. A few days later he returned and admitted that the rabbi had been right. What is that special spice you have?" he asked. Rabbi Joshua ben Hananiah smiled and answered, "It's called *Shabbat*."

SWEET & SOUR MEATBALL *CHOLENT*
(in a crock pot)

My niece, Debbie, is a beiryeh *(best translation -- superwoman). She's a* rebbetzin, *(a rabbi's wife) and a principal. She's a good cook, too!*

1 onion, diced	2 lbs. chopped meat
2 stalks celery	1/2 cup sweet wine
2-3 carrots	3/4 cup orange juice
1/4 cup beans	3 T. ketchup
1/2 cup barley	3/4-1 cup water
4-5 potatoes	1 t. garlic
1 sweet potato	salt & pepper (to taste)

Saute diced onion until translucent. Drain and put onion in bottom of crock pot. Layer chopped celery and carrots, barley and beans, diced sweet and white potatoes and meatballs. Mix wine, orange juice, ketchup and garlic. Stir well and add to crock pot. Add enough water so that approximately 1/2 - 3/4 of mixture is covered. Salt and pepper to taste. Cover. Cook on high at least one hour. Leave on low setting for the rest of *Shabbat*.

BOILED BEEF *CHOLENT*

2 lbs. beef or flanken
1/2 lb. celery root
1 parsnip
1 onion
1 kohlrabi
1 tomato

1 summer squash
a few grains of saffron
(optional)
salt & pepper (to taste)
1/2 cup chopped
parsley
water

Put all ingredients into a heavy pot and cover with hot water. Bring to a boil and place in oven. This *cholent* must be served with horseradish, dill pickles or mustard. Otherwise, it's quite bland. This is definitely not my favorite *cholent*, but many enjoy it.

LAMB *CHOLENT*

2 cups lima beans   2 cloves garlic, minced
2 lamb shanks   salt & pepper (to taste)
2 onions, sliced   1/2 t. ginger
3 T. oil   water

Soak the beans overnight in water to cover. Bring
to a boil and cook 30 minutes. Drain. Brown the
lamb and onions in the oil. Add the garlic, seasonings, and water. Cover and cook over low heat for
2 1/2 hours or until lamb and beans become tender. Add a little more water and place in low oven.

RAQUEL'S *CHOLENT* WITH BRISKET

A favorite of our talented daughter, Raquel. Our oldest is an educator par excellence, *a rabbi's wife and most importantly, mother of our darlings, Benjamin and Eliana!*

3 lbs. brisket
2 cups lima beans
3 onions, diced
3 T. oil or fat
salt & pepper (to taste)

1/4 t. ginger (optional)
1 cup barley
2 T. flour
2 t. paprika

Soak the beans overnight in water to cover. Drain. Use a heavy saucepan or Dutch oven and brown the meat and onions in the fat. Sprinkle with the salt, pepper and ginger. Add the beans and barley and sprinkle with the flour and paprika. Add enough boiling water to cover one inch above the mixture. Cover tightly.

Come For *Cholent*

Come For *Cholent*

SWEET AND SOUR TONGUE *CHOLENT*

Fresh tongue   1/2 cup water
2/3 cup brown sugar   3 or 4 prunes
2 onions (chopped   3 or 4 apricots
   fine)   1/4 cup raisins
2 T. lemon juice   1 cup small lima beans
2 cans tomato sauce (8   1/2 cup barley
   oz.)   water to cover

Mix brown sugar, onions, lemon juice, tomato
sauce and water. Bring to boil and add fruit and
raisins. Pour over tongue and beans and bake.
Prior to serving, peel skins off tongue and slice and
return to pot.

SAUSAGE *CHOLENT*

2 cups chick peas
2 lbs. beef (stew meat)
1 onion, chopped
water

3 carrots, diced
1 1/2 inch sausage,
   diced
salt & pepper (to taste)

Soak the chick peas overnight. Drain and add the water. Simmer on low heat for about an hour. Add the remaining ingredients.

South Americans brought this cholent to Israel and often add additional vegetables in season.

SHOULDER OF LAMB *CHOLENT*

1 4-5 lb. shoulder of
  lamb
2 cloves garlic
3 T. oil
4 sprigs mint
dash chili powder

1/2 cup white wine
5 potatoes, peeled and
  quartered
1 cup kidney beans
salt & pepper (to taste)
water to cover

Rub the lamb with garlic. Brown in hot oil. Put into a pot and sprinkle with seasonings. Place mint sprigs over the lamb and add the wine. Place potatoes and beans around the lamb.

Variation: The Jews of Alsace use the above recipe but add the following: raisins, dried pears, apricots, a whiff of rosemary and 2 T. of sugar. They omit the chili powder from this variation.

HAMBURGER *CHOLENT*

1 lb. ground beef
2 T. oil or fat
1 cup beans
1 cup chick peas
4 onions, diced
1 clove garlic, chopped

1/2 cup barley
8 medium-sized pota
   toes, halved
salt & pepper (to taste)
water

Roll ground beef into a ball. Put all the ingredients in a large heavy saucepan. Cover with boiling water and bring to the boil. Set over a very low heat or in a very slow oven (225°) and cook, covered, overnight. Do not stir up *cholent*.

A friend told me that her mother told her that this recipe is from Italy and is 500 years old. It has different names in different places -- shalet, sholet, sholend or chunt!

PINE NUT *CHOLENT*

2 cups ground beef
1 cup pine nuts
1/2 cup chopped green
   peppers

dash of cinnamon
salt & pepper (to taste)
cooking oil
grape juice (as desired)

Add the chopped green peppers, dash of cinnamon and salt and pepper to the meat and stir in the pine nuts. Brown in oil and sprinkle with grape juice. Wrap in foil and place in any *cholent*.

CHICKEN AND KASHA *CHOLENT*

My brother Alan, the doctor, claims this is a terrific cure for whatever ails you. Of course, my sister-in-law Liz still singes her chickens (to remove remaining pin feathers) over a lit candle melted to her kitchen sink! You have to see it to believe it!

1 cup kasha (whole)	1 cup celery, diced
1 chicken (pullet)	oil
2 onions, diced	salt & pepper (to taste)

In a 4-quart pot, saute onion and celery in oil. Add chicken and steam for 30-45 minutes. Add kasha, seasonings and water. Cook for approximately 20 minutes over a medium heat. Before *Shabbat*, add hot water to pot so that kasha doesn't dry out overnight.

VEAL *CHOLENT*

2 lbs. veal, in chunks	2 cloves garlic, minced
1 cup red kidney beans	salt & pepper (to taste)
2 onions, sliced	water
3 T. fat	

Soak the beans overnight in water to cover.
Bring to a boil and cook 30 minutes. Drain.
Brown the veal and onions in the fat. Add the
garlic, salt, pepper, and water. Cover and place
in 200^0 oven.

PUPIK CHOLENT*

Same as VEAL *CHOLENT*. Substitute 1 1/2 lbs.
pupik for veal.

"SPARE PARTS" *CHOLENT*

Same as VEAL *CHOLENT*. Substitute chicken
giblets (necks, *pupiks* and wings).

TURKEY *CHOLENT*

Same as VEAL *CHOLENT*. Substitute 2 lbs.
turkey cutlets or parts.

DUCK *CHOLENT*

Same as VEAL *CHOLENT*. Substitute 2-3 lbs.
duck.

*Yiddish for belly-button, but refers to a chicken's
stomach.

Come For *Cholent*   35

My research also led me to recipes for *cholent* with
Brains and Udder *Cholent*. Sorry, I couldn't bring
myself to include them. Especially the udder *cholent*
... "Slash the udder to release the milk. It must be
kashered in a vessel for udder only. Cover the
udder with boiling water, then..."

CHAPTER V

INTERNATIONAL CHOLENT

Beef *Cholent* with *Flohmentzimmes*
Fruited *Cholent*
Irish *Cholent*
...From Johannesburg, South Africa
...From London
Oriental *Cholent*
Algerian *Cholent* -- *Ḥamim Dfina*
Egyptian *Cholent* -- *Ḥamim Ferik*
Moroccan (Scheena), or *Cholent*
Greek *Cholent* -- *Stifatho*
Italian *Cholent* -- *Ḥamim Di Fagiolo*
Iraqi *Cholent* I and II
Stuffed Pumpkin *Cholent*

•In North Africa *cholent* is called *dafina* and also *shahine.*

CHOLENT NOTES

We are definitely in the midst of a *cholent* revival. Everytime I mentioned to anyone that I was writing a *cholent* cookbook, the response was overwhelmingly enthusiastic. No doubt if a convention of *cholent* lovers was organized there would be a tremendous response. What accounts for it? No one knows for sure. Perhaps, in part, a return to our roots and that more people are observing tradition. Possibly due to the convenience, economy and desirability of one-pot meals. When rediscovered, *cholent* is new yet traditional, filling yet healthful, gourmet yet earthy.

Best of all, *cholent* is easy to prepare for even the inexperienced cook. It can also be stretched to feed many extra guests. It can be re-heated without drying out in today's microwave "lifestyle." It is guaranteed to provide interesting dinner conversation and provoke nostalgic churnings. I have never served it without hearing a guest's secret family recipe or learning of a special *Shabbat* remembrance.

Cholent has been a popular dish throughout the world. For example, Ashkenazi Jews[1] prepare the traditional beef, bones, barley, beans, potatoes, and onions, and season with paprika.

[1]An Ashkenazi is a Jew whose ancestral roots are in central or Eastern Europe. Ashkenaz literally is Germany in Yiddish.

Sephardi Jews[2] often use lamb instead of beef and rice instead of barley. Syrian Jews place the mixture inside a hollowed-out pumpkin or squash. Oriental Jews prefer chicken instead of beef, and often add chicken gizzards and season with cardamon and mint. Afghani Jews season their *cholent* with cinnamon and add fresh quinces. North Africans often add chickpeas and kasha. In Turkey and North Africa there is a tradition of placing eggs in their shells within the *cholent*. Even with the wide range of ingredients and seasonings, all *cholent* requires ingredients that can endure lengthy, slow cooking. Most Jewish communities have in common a desire to add a *knaidel* (dumpling), *kugel* (pudding), or stuffed *kishke* (intestine) within the *cholent* pot.

Most fascinating in my research to find the perfect *cholent* was the realization (however unscientific) that each *cholent* is a universe unto itself. I wrote the Regional *Cholent* in America section on a Seattle to New York plane trip after having discovered that my friends on both coasts were willing to contribute their recipes but were also searching for new *cholent* ideas and recipes from other locales. In addition to seeking new flavors and taste sensations, their desire was also to connect to the past, to rekindle a fondly remembered tradition.

---

[2]Sephardi Jews are Jews whose ancestors lived for centuries in the Iberian peninsula until the expulsion of Jews from Spain by Queen Isabella's Edict of Expulsion in 1492. Subsequently, these Jews settled, for the most part, in the Mediterranean countries, especially Turkey and Greece. Most Jews in America are of Ashkenazi origin. In Israel today, the majority is Sephardi.

Come For *Cholent*

BEEF *CHOLENT* WITH *FLOHMENTZIMMES*
(PRUNES OR APRICOTS)

*This dish may be from the 11th or 12th century in Italy.
It became a favorite in North Africa and the Middle East.
The Italians claim* cholent *comes from the Italian word*
"caldo," *warm. It was cooked overnight in the village
baker's oven and brought home after the morning
synagogue service. Since observant Jews would not
carry things beyond their household (constituting work
on* Shabbat*) an* "eruv" *was put around the village to
make it "one home." (An* eruv *is the enclosure of an area
to make it one domain.)*

2 lbs. beef (cut into
  chunks)
2 lbs. sweet potatoes
  or yellow turnips
1 lb. prunes or dried
  apricots

salt & pepper (to taste)
5 T. brown sugar
  and/or honey
juice of 1 lemon
water

In a casserole, alternate layers of meat with layers
of sweet potatoes and prunes. Repeat until used
up. Mix the salt, pepper, sugar or honey and lemon
juice with enough water to cover the ingredients.
Cover the pot and bring to a boil, then reduce heat
to very low and cook for at least 2 hours, prior to
Shabbat.

FRUITED *CHOLENT*

This is a favorite version from Central and Eastern Europe.

2 lbs. brisket
1 lb. yellow turnips
  and/or carrots
1 lb. potatoes
juice of 1 lemon

1 lb. prunes
salt & pepper (to taste)
5 T. honey
water

In a heavy saucepan, arrange the meat with the turnips, potatoes and prunes. Mix together the salt, pepper, honey and lemon juice and add to meat mixture. Add sufficient water to cover the meat and vegetables. Cover, bring to a boil and then cook over low heat several hours and let it remain to simmer over *Shabbat*.

You may substitute sweet potatoes for turnips, dried apricots for prunes, and brown sugar for honey. All three or any one or two will produce delightful results.

IRISH* *CHOLENT*

2 lbs. lamb stew meat with bone	5 potatoes, peeled and cut in eighths
1/2 lb. carrots (cut in rounds)	2 T. flour
	1/4 cup oil
2 turnips (cut in small rounds)	1 bouillon cube
	salt & pepper (to taste)
small button onions (as desired)	water

Dredge lamb in flour and brown in oil. Dissolve bouillon cube in small amount of hot water and add to oil. Place lamb and vegetables in large roaster, add seasonings and water to cover.

Sofia, our cleaning lady, told me about this one. She isn't Irish and doesn't speak English but I tried it and it was superb! I wonder what Irish means in Polish!

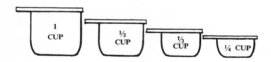

CHOLENT NO. 1

...From London

"Place 2 lbs. red haricot beans in a heavy pot with chopped parsley, 2 chopped onions, clove of garlic, pepper, cinnamon, a few cloves, salt, 3 table-spoons brown sugar and a fat boiling chicken. Cover with sufficient red wine and place in a low oven to simmer."

This recipe, and the following one, came to me from the Viniks of Birmingham, Alabama, who were vacationing at the same resort in Long Branch, New Jersey. Their car battery died, my husband rescued them, they noticed my manuscript on the back seat and the next thing I knew....

CHOLENT NO. 2

...From Johannesburg, South Africa

"Use your heaviest pot, a Dutch oven or preferably a copper pot. Grease the pot well with chicken fat. Now prepare 3 lbs. small potatoes, all the same size more or less, grated onion which you should mix with chicken fat, flour, salt, pepper and other seasonings. Set down a layer of potatoes, sprinkle with the flour mixture, place a nice piece of flank or lean brisket on top of the potatoes, sprinkle again with the flour mixture, cover with the rest of the potatoes, sprinkle more of the flour mixture over this, add water to cover the potatoes and bring the ingredients to the boil on top of the stove. Place the dish in a low oven to cook and forget about it. Be sure that the dish is very tightly covered. Do not succumb to the temptation of peeking. A few hours towards the end of cooking you may become inquisitive to see if more water and seasoning is needed. When ready, turn the whole thing onto a platter and serve."

ORIENTAL *CHOLENT*

1 1/2 cups dry chick
   peas (garbanzo
   beans)
4-5 potatoes
1-2 sweet potatoes
1 lb. flanken
1/2 cup brown rice

1/2 cup white rice
olive oil
3 dates
Season with: paprika,
   cinnamon, tumeric,
   salt, pepper, garlic
water

Soak chick peas overnight. Mix rice in bowl with olive oil, salt, pepper, and seasonings. Tie the mixture firmly in a cheesecloth bag and place in pot with all other ingredients and boil. When serving, remove cheesecloth bag and serve rice separately. It will have absorbed all the delicious flavors of the *cholent*.

ALGERIAN *CHOLENT* -- *ḤAMIM DFINA*

The *Dfina* ("hidden" *Cholent*)

1 cup chick peas	1 very small chili
1 1/2 lbs. fat beef	pepper (or 1 t. chili
1 lb. bones	sauce)
4 cloves garlic	1 pimento
1 large onion	salt & pepper (to taste)
6 eggs in their shells	water

The *Kouclas* (An Algerian *matzah* ball)

2 eggs	1 onion
salt & pepper (to taste)	1 cup breadcrumbs
1 T. chopped parsley	

Soak the chick peas for a few hours. Drain. In an earthenware casserole put the fat beef, bones, garlic, onion, eggs in their shells, chick peas, chili pepper or sauce, pimento and salt and pepper. Cover with water.

For the *kouclas*, combine the eggs, salt and pepper, parsley, chopped onion and breadcrumbs. Shape into a ball and add to the casserole. Close the casserole firmly and either simmer overnight or put into an oven.

EGYPTIAN *CHOLENT* -- *ḤAMIM FERIK*

The unusual feature of the following cholent *is the use of unshelled eggs. They come out a deep brown outside and inside and are soft and flavorful.*

2 lbs. brisket of beef
2 cups green wheat or
    burghul (cracked
    wheat)
6 eggs, unshelled

1 calf's foot (optional)
salt & pepper (to taste)
2 cloves garlic
water

Brown the meat in a heavy pot. Put it on a bed of wheat and surround with the eggs in their shells and the bones. Put in the seasoning and garlic and cover with water. Bring to a slow boil. Cover tightly and place in oven.

MOROCCAN (SCHEENA) OR *CHOLENT*

This Moroccan recipe is from Faye Davis, a dear friend now living in Bellevue, Washington.

1 lb. chickpeas (gar-
banzo) soaked over
night, drained
6-7 pitted dates or 2 T.
brown sugar
2 lbs. chuck roast
(boneless)
10-15 small-medium
red potatoes, peeled
4 large sweet potatoes,
peeled and cut up

8-10 eggs (washed)
1 1/2 cups long grain
rice
1 t. saffron
1/4 cup oil + 1/4 cup
oil
2 heads garlic separate
cloves or remove
outer skin

Layer first 5 ingredients in given order, salt and pepper to taste, add 1/4 cup oil and 3/4 of garlic cloves. Add water to level of eggs. Wash and drain rice. Put in small bowl or in a pocket make of tin foil. Add saffron, salt and pepper, the rest of garlic cloves, 1/4 cup oil, cover with water and place in a corner of the pan amongst the other ingredients. If using a crock pot, cook on high for first 3 hours. Then on low until the next day, or in oven at 200⁰F. Add water if necessary.

GREEK *CHOLENT -- STIFATHO*

A dish reportedly made in Israel 2,000 years ago.

2 lbs. tender beef
1/2 cup red wine
1 cup very small
  onions
4 T. cooking oil
1/2 cup margarine
1/2 cup tomato paste
  or ketchup

1 cinnamon stick
dash of saffron
  (optional)
1/2 t. pickling spice
water
salt & pepper (to taste)
1 T. vinegar

(The meat may be marinated in the wine over-night, but that is not required.)
Cut the meat into 2 inch cubes. Peel the onions. Brown the meat in the hot oil, then add the margarine and remove the meat to a casserole. Brown the onions and set aside. Cook the tomato paste in the remaining margarine and pour over the meat with the remaining ingredients (except the onions). Bring to a boil on high heat, then reduce to simmer. Close the casserole tightly.

ITALIAN *CHOLENT -- ḤAMIM DI FAGIOLO*

Italian ḥamim *(the Hebrew word for hot) uses a highly spiced tomato sauce.*

1 lb. beans
1 cup tomato sauce (as
 spicy as desired)
4 cups water
2 lbs. minced meat
3 eggs

3 T. breadcrumbs
2 T. minced parsley
3 T. oil for frying
1 onion, chopped
salt & pepper (to taste)

Soak the beans overnight. Put the drained beans in a heavy pot with the tomato sauce and the water and bring to a boil. Mix the chopped meat, egg, breadcrumbs, and parsley and form into 4 or 5 balls (which are cut up for serving). Fry the meatballs in the oil with the onion. When the sauce in the beans begins to thicken, season to taste and put the meat, oil, and onion on top. Cover tightly.

IRAQI *CHOLENT* I

1 cup lima beans
1 chicken, cut-up
  (3-4 lbs.)
1/2 cup rice
10 large tomatoes,
  diced

3 T. oil for frying
dash of cinnamon and
  cardamon
salt & pepper (to taste)
5 medium potatoes
water to cover

Fry the rice in the oil until golden. Add four of the diced tomatoes with a dash of cinnamon, cardamon, and salt. Put the washed and soaked beans in a pot with the chicken. Surround with potatoes. Sprinkle with cinnamon, cardamon, salt and pepper. Top with the remaining tomatoes. Cover with water. Cover well and simmer overnight. Serves 6.

IRAQI *CHOLENT* II

1 cup navy beans
1 cup chick peas
1 whole roasting
  chicken
1/2 cup rice
3 T oil
10 large tomatoes

cumin, salt & pepper
1 cup burghul (or more
  rice)
1 lb. squash, winter or
  summer, or pumpkin
water to cover

Skin the chicken from below the wings to include the wings and skin of the neck. Fry the rice and add half of the diced tomatoes sprinkled with cumin, salt and pepper. Fill the cavity of the skin with rice about 1/3 full and sew up. Put the beans and chick peas in a saucepan with the skin, chicken, and the stuffed skin next to it. Surround with burghul and vegetables. Sprinkle with more seasonings. Top with the remaining tomatoes. Cover with water and put on stove to simmer.

STUFFED PUMPKIN *CHOLENT*
A Syrian delicacy!

1 whole pumpkin or
   squash (or large slice)
1 lb. cubed chicken
   breast
1/2 cup rice
1 can stewed tomatoes
   (10 oz.)

1/2 cup diced onions
1 cup kidney beans
1/4 cup oil
4 cubed potatoes
cinnamon
salt & pepper (to taste)
water to cover

Line roaster or heavy pan with heavy-duty foil. Slice off top and remove seeds from pumpkin or squash. Mix all ingredients and stuff in hollowed out shell. (If desired, chicken and onion may be sauteed in oil prior to mixing). Add 2" water. Cover with foil and tightly seal edges.

CHAPTER VI

VERY SPECIAL CHOLENT

Chocolate *Cholent*
"Death" by *Cholent*
Shirley's *Cholent*
Cholent Stroganoff

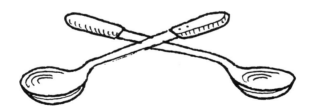

•My husband says you should eat *cholent* with peanut butter!

REGIONAL *CHOLENT* COOKING IN AMERICA!

Pacific Northwest

It only stands to reason that just as salmon, due to its abundance and delicious taste, is utilized in the making of Pacific Northwest gefilte fish, Pacific Northwest *cholent* takes on flavors of readily available ingredients that add to the special *ta'am* (flavor) of the Northwest.

However, while cooking in Seattle for over 18 years, I experimented with attempts at salmon and fish *cholent* but never felt quite satisfied. As a result, you won't find fish *cholent* anywhere in this collection. However, the addition of numerous varieties of Northwest mushrooms enhanced many of my *cholent* recipes, especially those including barley. Being somewhat of a mushroom addict myself, my children relish them, too. So if "shrooms" are your thing, experiment by adding 1/2 lb. of dried or fresh oriental mushrooms, straw mushrooms, wild mushrooms or any available variety. You may wish to cut back on beans to make room in the cholent pot. You'll find sauteing mushrooms prior to adding them to *cholent* produces a more succulent flavor. Remember, fresh mushrooms cook down considerably.

Northeast

Only in the Northeast corridor have I been able to find packages of beans labelled "All In One Shabbos Chulent Mix." Inexpensively priced and packaged in convenient one pound packages of cranberry beans, red kidney and white beans, they eliminate all decisions on which beans to select for inclusion.

Of course, nowhere is kosher eating as facile as in New York. Delicious *cholent* is available in many kosher restaurants as an entree or as a "side dish." Take-out *cholent* also appears on many menus. A congregant once asked us if it were permissible to eat *cholent* during the week, to which I replied, "Why not? But don't expect it to taste like *Shabbos cholent!*"

Midwestern *Cholent*

My mother made a Missouri *cholent* that was the most delicious I ever tasted. I can close my eyes to this day and smell the aroma in our home over *Shabbat*. Mom's mixture of meat, beans and potatoes came to Kansas City via Bereza Kartuzka, Poland. My father, originally from Beranavich, often offered ideas for special additions. His favorite was adding *gribenes* (fried chicken skins -- recipe appears on page 69) to each serving, sprinkling them over his plate like salad croutons. So, if you were expecting a true midwestern *cholent* and not one emanating from Poland, *mea culpa!*

Mexican *Cholent* or *Cholent* Con Chili

My husband's first pulpit took us to Mexico City, D.F. We were young enough and our bodies strong enough to enjoy adding dried hot chili pepper pods to *cholent*. While not in the special league of "fire eaters," a small amount added a zip and zing to our standard, basic *cholent*. It was always interesting to observe the enthusiasm or finesse of our North American guests in handling it. In contrast, our local congregants often requested additional chili for sprinkling on individual servings. Our favorite chilies included fiery hot cayenne, Tabasco, scotch bonnet and bird chilies. I'm told that *cholent* cooks in Bombay who grew up with Parsi Indian food routinely add chili curries to everything! Vinegar and sugar at the table, added to taste, adds a touch of sweet and sour, which helps balance flavor and "tones down the heat." Oh yes, when it comes to taste buds and appetites, there are indeed differences.

South

My southern friends and relatives tell me that garlic is their secret ingredient in cooking. Garlic has been a dietary staple for thousands of years and has also had magical qualities imputed to it. There is even a fair amount of scientific evidence, we are told, that some of those magical properties have a basis in fact. Recent findings indicate garlic may lower blood pressure, reduce the risk of blood clotting, lower cholesterol and even inhibit the growth of some cancer cells. Some researchers say that sulfur-containing compounds are responsible for garlic's biological activity. They credit allicin (a compound) with lowering cholesterol. Allicin is produced when fresh garlic is cut. The amount one needs to eat for all of these benefits is yet unclear. I like it best added to *cholent* with a tomato-red base. It's certainly more appealing than the "magic bullets" -- oat bran -- of the 80s! And, eating it certainly beats wearing it around the neck. So, enjoy, but don't forget the breath mints!

CHOCOLATE *CHOLENT*

I invented this cholent *during the years my husband had a pulpit in Mexico City, D.F. Then I called it* Cholent Con Mole *or* Cholent Olé. *It now sounds more appealing as Chocolate* Cholent!

2 lbs. chuck roast	1 lb. red pinto beans
2 T. oil	(soaked overnight)

Brown meat on all sides in hot oil, turning frequently.

Prepare chocolate sauce:

1 medium onion (grated)	2 squares unsweetened chocolate
2 cloves garlic (minced)	1/2 cup peanut butter
2 T. oil	1/4 cup yellow corn meal
3 cups beef bouillon	1/2 t. chili powder (or, to taste)
1 can (8 oz.) tomato sauce	2 T. sesame seeds (toasted)
1 t. cumin (ground)	

Saute onion and garlic in hot oil in large skillet until onion is lightly browned. Stir in bouillon, tomato sauce, chocolate (broken), and peanut butter. Stir until chocolate is melted and peanut butter is thoroughly blended. Thoroughly mix together corn meal, chili powder, sesame seeds, and cumin. Add slowly to the bouillon mixture, stirring constantly over low heat until well blended. Bring to a boil, turn heat low and simmer about 5 minutes. Place all ingredients in a large heavy pot or crock pot. Add water only if chocolate sauce does not cover meat and beans.

P.S. After this lunch, don't plan on going out to eat Saturday night!

"DEATH" BY *CHOLENT*

A favorite of my son-in-law, "Rabbi Bill," a gourmet chef. Who else would give me a recipe like this!

2 lbs. chuck (cubed)
1 lb. onion (chopped)
8-10 cloves garlic, finely chopped (more if you love garlic)
1-2 cans of your favorite beer (probably 2)
1 lb. *cholent* beans
1 deli *kishka* roll (cut up into 1 1/2" chunks)
1/2 lb. pastrami (optional, but don't leave it out!)
6 potatoes (peeled and quartered)
2-3 T. oil
1 t. paprika
salt & pepper (to taste)
water to cover

Saute onions and garlic in oil until translucent and remove. Brown meat. Add sauteed onions and garlic and remaining ingredients and put in large dutch oven. Hmmm... the aroma alone will "kill" you.

SHIRLEY'S* *CHOLENT*

Cut into 1 1/2 inch cubes any meat you would like -- beef, veal or lamb. Pare, cut in half and add vegetables of your choice such as potatoes, onions, carrots or celery as a base, and other vegetables as available such as mushrooms, green pepper, zucchini, turnips, or peas. Throw in some dried beans (whatever makes you happy). Pour one (or maybe 2) cans of onion soup over it all. Add a clove of garlic and place in oven. Before serving, add salt & pepper to taste, cover with water. You can't go wrong -- it always tastes great!

My sister-in-law Shirley can do anything! With this recipe, who needs a cookbook!

CHOLENT STROGANOFF

This cholent will look like a real stroganoff made with cream. It will also taste like cream. You may show your guests this recipe if they need convincing!*

1 1/2 lbs. shoulder steak	Gravy:
	4 cups beef gravy (or
flour for coating	from boullion cubes)
3 onions chopped	2 T. flour
1 lb. mushrooms,	1 t. paprika
chopped	6 T. ketchup
1 clove garlic, crushed	1 T. worchestershire or
salt & pepper (to taste)	tabasco sauce
6 T. margarine	4 T. mayonnaise

Cut meat into 1/2-inch thick strips. Dip the meat in flour and season. Fry the onions and mushrooms and garlic in margarine for 5 minutes. Add the meat and cook 5 additional minutes.

To make the gravy, drain off the juice from the meat and vegetables and add enough beef stock to make 4 cups. Blend in the flour smoothly. Add the paprika, ketchup and worchestershire sauce. Cook until thick. Keep warm over *Shabbat*, lowest heat. Remove from heat and add mayonnaise before serving.

*According to Kosher dietary laws no dairy products may be combined with meat. Clever combinations of ingredients may be used to approximate a desired taste or flavor.

CHAPTER VII

EXOTIC CHOLENT

Pharaoh's Wheel *Cholent*
Alisa's Salsa *Cholent*
Cholent with *Shmaltz* and *Gribenes*
Stuffed *Miltz Cholent*
Cholent with Wine and Olives
Western Chuck Wagon *Cholent*

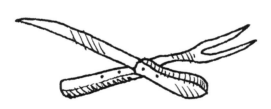

•*Cholent* or *shulent* may derive from the Yiddish *shul ende* meaning the end of the Saturday synagogue service.

THE *CHOLENT* CHALLENGE

or
FINDING THE RIGHT TITLE FOR A *CHOLENT* COOKBOOK

You may rate the following on a scale of 1-5:

Cholent in a Chafing dish
The Cholent Champion
Change to Cholent
Cheer for Cholent
Cholent Cheer
Choose Cholent
Choosing Cholent
Cholent by Choice
Chant for Cholent
The *Cholent* Channel
Cholent in the Chapel
No Charcoal in the *Cholent*
Don't Char the *Cholent*
Chard *Cholent*
Chervil *Cholent*
Be Charitable About *Cholent*
Cholent Charm
How Charming the *Cholent*
The Charm of *Cholent*
Charting *Cholent*
A *Cholent* Chart
The *Cholent* Chase
A Chaser for *Cholent*
A *Cholent* Chase
Cholent for the Chaste

CHOLENT PREVIEWS

• The Chaste Chaplain Was Chastised for Chanting About *Cholent* in the Chapel with Chimes

• A Chat About *Cholent*
The Frugal Gourmet interviews this author!

• *Cholent* Chatter
Oprah Winfrey invites me to her show!

• Checking Out *Cholent*
A new take-out store!

• No Cheating With *Cholent*
A new diet book!

• *Cholent* Can Be Cheap
Feeding 20 for the price of beans!

• Here's *Cholent* In Your Cheek
Behavior modification therapy!

• A Child of *Cholent*
Love is not enough!

• Chow *Cholent*
Fortune cookies for dessert!

PHARAOH'S WHEEL *CHOLENT*

An Israeli cholent *symbolic of the Wheel of Pharaoh's fate is eaten on* Shabbat Beshalaḥ *(the Sabbath during which in all synagogues the Biblical portion describing the exodus from Egypt, is read). The sauce is reminiscent of the Red Sea; the black raisins and white nuts swimming in the gravy represent the Egyptians and their steeds. Baked in a round casserole, reminiscent of the wheels of the charioteers.*

1/2 lb. broad egg noodles	6 oz. sausage or salami (thinly sliced)
1 1/2 cups meat gravy	1/2 cup pine nuts
1/2 cup raisins	

Boil the noodles 5 minutes and drain. In a greased casserole put alternate layers of the noodles, meat gravy, and sausage sprinkled with raisins and pine nuts. The top layer should be of noodles, with a circular border of sausage. Heat for 20 minutes only and place in oven on lowest temperature. This *cholent* should have plenty of gravy. Do not add water to cover as in other *cholent* recipes.

ALISA'S SALSA *CHOLENT*

My daughter, the cantor, can sing anything. I think salsa music inspired this zesty cholent.

1 lb. black beans (washed and picked over)
1 cup chopped onion
1 tomato, chopped
1/2 cup green pepper, minced
1/4 cup cilantro
1 T. balsamic vinegar
4 T. olive oil
1 T. sugar

6 cups chicken soup (instant) or chicken stock
2 t. soy sauce
1 1/2 t. oregano
1/4 t. lemon pepper seasoning
1 clove garlic, minced
1 lb. skinless breast of turkey cut into chunks
salt & pepper (to taste)

Soak the beans overnight in cold water. Drain. Heat the oil in a large, heavy pot and saute the onion until golden. Next add the remaining ingredients. Serve with sprigs of fresh cilantro for decoration.

CHOLENT WITH SHMALTZ AND GRIBENES

(RENDERED CHICKEN FAT AND FRIED CHICKEN SKINS)

3 lbs. of brisket, short ribs or flanken
2 cups dried lima beans
3 medium onions, peeled and diced
1/4 cup *shmaltz* (rendered chicken fat)*

6 cloves garlic, crushed
salt & pepper (to taste)
1/4 cup barley
3 or 4 large russet or Idaho potatoes, peeled and quartered
water to cover
Gribenes (fried chicken skins)

Soak lima beans in water to cover for 4 hours or overnight. Saute the onions in *shmaltz* or oil in the bottom of a heavy stockpot or Dutch oven large enough to hold all the ingredients and still leave room for beans and barley to expand. Cook, stirring, until onions begin to brown, add garlic and seasonings and cook one minute more. Remove half the mixture and reserve. Drain the lima beans and place them in the bottom of the pot on top of the sauteed onions. Sprinkle on barley and layer on the potatoes with the reserved onions. Place the meat over all. Add enough water to cover the meat by 2 inches. Cover the pot very tightly with a layer of foil and a lid on top and place on *blech* or in oven. Sprinkle *gribenes* on cholent prior to serving. Pass around extra gribenes to add as desired.

A recipe for shmaltz *and* gribenes *follows.*

SHMALTZ AND GRIBENES

Rendered chicken fat and fried skins!

Rendered fat from a chicken or goose was to European Jews what olive oil is to Mediterranean people. Oil was rare and expensive, forcing a Jewish homemaker to find an available and thrifty substitute. Although fat is avoided today by many people because of what we know about cholesterol and the causes of heart disease, this cholent book would not be complete without inclusion of this delicacy. Anyway, my husband's Bobie and Zadie lived well into their nineties while dining on shmaltz and gribenes at least once a week. Those who have never tried it should know that its flavor is never to be forgotten!

Remove as much chicken fat as possible along with some of the skin from the chickens. Cut the fat and skin into small pieces. Save in plastic bags in your freezer until you have 3-4 cups of chicken fat and skins and you are ready to render the fat and fry the skins. Place 3-4 cups of raw chicken fat and skins in a large, heavy skillet or frying pan. Cook over moderate heat until the fat liquifies and the solid pieces become much smaller and turn golden brown. Add a medium onion (diced). When the onion and skins have become crisp and very brown, remove from heat. Remove the *gribenes* with a slotted spoon. Add one teaspoon salt to the rendered fat, stir and let stand until slightly cooked but still liquid. You should have approximately one cup *shmaltz*. Save in a glass jar and refrigerate or freeze. It will last indefinitely either way. Keep *gribenes* covered in the refrigerator. They may be added to *cholent*, of course, but are also delicious added to chopped liver and mashed potatoes!

STUFFED *MILTZ CHOLENT*

1 *miltz* (cow spleen)
4 slices *hallah*, crust
  removed
1 onion, chopped
3 T. margarine
1 t. garlic powder
4 large onions, sliced

4 large potatoes,
  quartered
4 large carrots, sliced
4 T. cooking oil
salt & pepper (to taste)
water to cover

With a long, sharp knife, make a pocket in the *miltz* almost from end to end. Soak bread in small amount of water and then squeeze dry. Fry the chopped onion in the margarine and mix with the bread and seasonings. Stuff into the *miltz* (not too full or it will split open) and sew up with needle and thread. Layer onions, potatoes and carrots in the bottom of the pot. Place *miltz* carefully on top and pour the oil over to cover. The *miltz* will pot roast as the water is absorbed.

CHOLENT WITH WINE AND OLIVES

4 onions, diced
1 large celery root,
  diced
3 parsnip roots, diced
1/2 lb. carrots, diced
4 T. olive oil
1 cup dry red wine
4 cloves garlic
2 bay leaves

2 T. chopped parsley
1 T. chopped dill
3 lbs. beef chuck
1/2 lb. black olives
4 large tomatoes
smoked sausage, thinly
  sliced (optional)
salt & pepper (to taste)
water to cover

Fry the onion, celery root, parsnips, and carrots in the oil for a few minutes. Add the wine, salt, pepper, garlic, and herbs. Simmer for a few minutes. Cool and pour over the meat to marinate. (Some cooks marinate overnight, but an hour in advance works nicely). Add remaining ingredients and cook. If you wish, the olives and smoked sausage may be added as a garnish when serving.

WESTERN CHUCK WAGON *CHOLENT*

This cholent *comes from sunny California, where else?*

6 red potatoes (halved)
1/2 lb. white beans
2 lbs. chuck roast (cut
   up)
1 cup salad oil
2 cups beer
1/4 cup lemon juice
salt & pepper (to taste)

2 cloves garlic
   (minced)
2 bay leaves
1 t. dry mustard
1 t. basil
1 t. oregano
1 t. thyme

Combine oil, beer, lemon juice, and seasonings and pour over meat. Refrigerate one hour. Place meat and beans in crock pot and add marinade. Add sufficient water to cover.

CHAPTER VIII

MISCELLANEOUS CHOLENT

2nd Avenue Deli *Cholent*
Kasha-Onion *Cholent*
Corn and Corned Beef *Cholent*
Carla's Rice and Mushroom *Cholent*
Lentil *Cholent*
Cholent with Black Bean Sauce
Cholent with Parsnips
Mildred Bellin's *Cholent* & Potato *Cholent*
"Instant" *Cholent*
David's *Helzel Cholent*

•Some say the only "cure" for *Cholent* is an Alka-Seltzer and a long nap!

P.S.

Cholent is a hearty meal and contains all the essential daily food group requirements plus vitamins.

The great lexicographer and father of modern spoken Hebrew, Eliezer Ben Yehuda used to say, when he had eaten of the gourmet dishes of Paris and longed for his home in Russia, "Give me a bowl of *Shabbos cholent*, peppered and with onions for this is the soul and savor of food."

It may be served solo without any additional courses. Or, it may be served as a side dish in lieu of starch.

Our family tradition is to precede it with a fresh salad or fruit cup and follow it with dessert, coffee, and tea. The Saturday noon meal begins with *Kiddush* (the blessing over the wine), *Hamotzi* (the blessing for Sabbath bread, *hallah*), and concludes with *birkat hamazon* (grace after the meal).

Cholent is most often eaten with a fork, however a soupier variety may require a spoon. It should never require a knife.

Our family's *cholent* etiquette includes the following verse:

- *HALLAH* WORKS GREAT FOR CLEANING YOUR *CHOLENT* PLATE!

2ND AVENUE DELI *CHOLENT*

Abe Lebewohl, now famous restaurateur can't believe how popular cholent *has become as a menu item.* "I've been in the restaurant business for 35 years and never served cholent before now. I had some leftover following a Kiddush I catered for a shule and offered it to my customers that evening. To my surprise, everyone loved it! We added it to our menus and can't believe the response." *Abe, who grew up in Williamsburg but now resides in New York, went on to describe an example of who orders* cholent. *"The popularity of* cholent *is 'blowing my mind.' You know you can usually tell when someone comes in, what they're going to order. In comes two stylishly dressed women who are clearly watching their diets. They order a half sandwich and a huge bowl of* cholent! *Everyone loves* cholent!" *Only one problem; Abe's recipe is for 180-200 people. He cooks it in a 20 gallon vat! He says he never measures anyway.* "Just pick the right size pot and fill it:

Lots of Yankee and red
  kidney beans
barley
sauteed onions and
  celery (diced)
carrots (diced)
kishke "bursts" (no
  casing -- just stuffing)

Long Island chef
  potatoes (white
  boiling potatoes)
flanken meat (cubed,
  no bone), or any rich
  meat
beef and chicken stock
salt & pepper (to taste)

Abe invites you in for a sample and offers a coupon for "a free portion of tantalizing cholent on your next visit." He also has this cookbook for sale!

2nd Avenue Deli is located at 156 Second Avenue. It's worth a trip to New York!

KASHA-ONION *CHOLENT*

6 medium onions,
  diced
1/4 cup vegetable oil
  or shmaltz
3 to 4 lbs. brisket
4 cloves garlic, crushed

2 cups dried lima
  beans (soaked over
  night)
salt & pepper (to taste)
2 cups kasha (whole or
  medium buckwheat
  groats)

Saute the onions in oil until they are lightly browned. Place the onions, meat, lima beans, garlic and salt into a large Dutch oven. Place the kasha on top and pour the water over everything, leaving 1-2 inches of water to cover. Cover tightly and place in oven.

When serving this style *cholent*, remove meat and slice and arrange on a large platter. Surround the sliced meat with the other *cholent* ingredients.

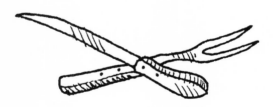

CORN AND CORNED BEEF *CHOLENT*

3-4 lbs. corned beef
(lean)
5-6 carrots, scraped
and quartered
3 parsnips, scraped
and quartered
2 medium heads green
cabbage, trimmed of
outer leaves and
quartered

6 large potatoes,
peeled and cut in
thirds
8 small white onions,
peeled and left whole
4 ears corn-on-the-cob,
shucked and cut into
thirds (or one large
can of whole corn,
drained)

Place corned beef in pot, add corn, potatoes and all other ingredients. Add enough water to cover the meat by 2 inches. Prior to serving, slice the corned beef and arrange on a platter. Surround with vegetables and pour over a little of the broth to keep everything moist. This *cholent* is delicious served with horseradish or mustard and plenty of good rye bread.

CARLA'S RICE & MUSHROOM *CHOLENT*

My niece Carla won the Betty Crocker Award for cooking in eighth grade! She says all her recipes include "bits and things your mom tells you, things you saw your Bobie *(Yiddish for grandma) do and things you just incorporate."*

2 cups rice (white, brown, wild, in any combination)
1 cup mushrooms (canned or fresh)
4 lbs. chuck or brisket
2 onions, sliced
2 T. fat
salt & pepper (to taste)
1 t. paprika
1/2 t. garlic powder
boiling water

Brown the meat and onions in the fat. Add the salt, pepper, paprika, garlic powder, and water. Cover loosely and cook over low heat 2 hours. Add the rice and mushrooms and a little more water, if necessary. Place in warm oven.

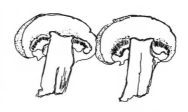

LENTIL *CHOLENT*

My mother-in-law brought this recipe from Raanana to San Diego, so you'd better try it! My sister-in-law, Bete, makes a Baltimorian version that's yummy. Enjoy!

2 cups lentils	salt & pepper (to taste)
1 cup navy beans	1 cup pearl barley
3 lbs. flanken	2 t. paprika
3 onions, diced	water
3 T. fat	

Soak the beans overnight in water (to cover). Drain. Use a heavy saucepan or crock pot and brown the meat and onions in the fat. Sprinkle with salt and pepper. Add the beans and barley and sprinkle with paprika. Add enough boiling water to cover 1 inch above the mixture. Cover tightly and place in 250^0 oven. When ready to serve, slice the meat and serve with beans and barley. Serves 8-10 people.

CHOLENT WITH BLACK BEAN SAUCE

2 cups black beans
3 lbs. flanken
2 onions, sliced
salt & pepper (to taste)
1 lb. marrow bones

3 carrots, diced
1 cup barley
1/2 cup dried mush-
   rooms
water

Soak the beans overnight in water to cover. Drain. Use a heavy baking dish or crock pot and begin layering with meat and onions. (Both may be browned first, in a small amount of oil, if desired.) Add the remaining ingredients and salt and pepper. Add boiling water to cover. Cover tightly and bake in a 250⁰ oven overnight. Serves 6-8.

CHOLENT WITH PARSNIPS

1 cup dried beans
4 T. oil
2 lbs. brisket or fat
   meat
2 onions, chopped
1 cup kasha

1 clove garlic, crushed
salt & pepper (to taste)
water
1 or 2 large parsnips,
   grated

Soak the beans overnight. Heat the oil and brown the meat in it. Remove the meat and lightly fry the onions. Fry the kasha for just a minute or two. In a heavy pot put the drained beans. Place the meat on the beans and surround with the kasha, onions, garlic, parsnips and seasonings. Cover with water and bring to a boil. Reduce heat and put in 200^0 oven.

MILDRED BELLIN'S *CHOLENT* & POTATO *CHOLENT*

1 cup dried lima or pea beans
2 quarts water
1/2 cut coarse barley
1 t. ground ginger

2 lbs. shortribs, plate, or brisket of beef
1/2 t. garlic powder
1 T. salt
1/4 t. black pepper

Since no cooking may be done on the Sabbath, this dish is begun early Friday morning. Soak the beans in the water at least 6 hours. Add remaining ingredients, bring to a boil, cover, and simmer for 30 minutes. Cut the meat into serving-sized pieces, and place, with the rest of the soup, in a large earthenware or iron casserole. Cover tightly and set in a very cool oven, no hotter than 250°F, until Saturday noon. *Cholent* was traditionally made in a coal stove with the fire banked, or sent to the baker to be completed in his cooled ovens. A well-regulated electric stove or roaster may be used instead with satisfactory results. This is served as a soup for 8.

Potato *Cholent*: Substitute 6 peeled and quartered medium potatoes for the barley.

Reprinted from The Original Jewish Cookbook *with permission of Bloch Publishing Company.*

"INSTANT" CHOLENT

If you just can't get enough of that succulent, savory cholent *and frequently crave it, this recipe is for you!*

Using the Basic, Scrumptious *Cholent* recipe on page 5, begin by boiling the bones and meat with seasonings for one hour. Skim, and add the remaining ingredients, lowering heat for an additional hour. Stir and place pot in oven for an additional 1 1/2 hours. Many recipes in this collection lend themselves to an "instant" cooking process.

As always, enjoy!

DAVID'S *HELZEL CHOLENT*

*Our close friend and former neighbor, David Palgon is
"fixated" on* helzel *(neck). Of course, he's eccentric in
many other ways too! He's been begging me to share my
recipe with him for years. So, for Esther, who loves to
"order in," Roger and Harriet, Ethel and Stan and the
Queens Gang -- Enjoy!*

1 whole goose neck (or
   several chicken necks
   sewn together)
1 onion, chopped
1/2 lb. ground chicken
1/4 cup fat (*shmaltz*)

1 cup chicken soup
1 egg
1 cup flour
1 garlic clove, crushed
salt, pepper, paprika

Chop or grind meat, onion and fat. Add remaining
ingredients and mix thoroughly. Sew together the
narrow end. Fill neck with the stuffing. Sew any
remaining openings.

Delicious baked in center of *cholent* pot (or may be
baked alone). Slice and serve.

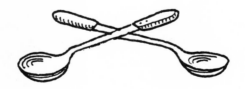

EDITH KLEIN'S CHOLENT

Edith Klein originally made this recipe in her native Hungary using smoked goose! Unable to readily obtain that delicacy today, she achieves a similar smoky flavor by using pastrami. Edith's husband, Murray, is an owner of my favorite food emporium -- Zabar's -- on 81st Street and Broadway in New York City.

1 lb. dried Great
  Northern beans
1/4 cup chicken fat or
  vegetable oil
2 large onions, chopped
3 shallots, chopped
3 cloves garlic, chopped
1/2 lb. pastrami, in one
  piece

2 1/2 lbs. boneless
  flanken or brisket (in
  2-inch chunks)
1 T. Hungarian
  paprika
1 T. honey
1/2 cup pearl barley
Salt & pepper (to taste)

Place beans in a bowl, cover with cold water to a depth of 2" and allow to soak at least 4 hours or overnight. Heat fat in a large, heavy casserole. Add onions and shallots and saute until golden. Stir in garlic and cook for about a minute. Remove vegetables from pan with a slotted spoon, draining well, and set aside. Brown chunks of beef lightly in the fat and remove them. Pre-heat oven to 400⁰. Cut pastrami into 1" cubes and stir into the fat, adding the paprika and honey. Return onions, shallots, garlic and beef to casserole. Stir in barley. Drain beans and add them. Add 6 cups boiling water to casserole. Cover and place in oven. Bake for 30 minutes. Reduce heat to 250⁰ and bake 30 minutes longer. Remove lid and season to taste with salt and pepper. Cover casserole with aluminum foil and replace the lid. Bake in oven 7-8 hours or overnight.

ABOUT THE AUTHOR

Kay Kantor Pomerantz is a talented lady. Her successful career in Jewish education has been marked by many honors and appointments. Most notably, a library in her name was established in Seattle, Washington, where she served as Executive Director of the Jewish Education Council for sixteen years. She currently serves as Assistant Director of the Department of Education in the United Synagogue of America. She is a rebbetzin and mother of four extraordinary children. She and her family reside in New York.

CATHY COULD HAVE COOKED CHOLENT!

Come For *Cholent*